Album of
Prehistoric
Man

ALBUM OF PREHISTORIC MAN

A PIECE OF broken rock, bits of ash, a few chunks of ancient bone—these things don't really add up to much. Most people would step around them without so much as a passing glance. Yet anthropologists, anatomists, archaeologists, chemists, and physicists—scientists of all kinds—are different. They might stop to examine these seemingly worthless bits, for in them can be read the story of the human race.

Like good detectives, scientists are persistent and patient in their investigation. Like good detectives, they examine even the smallest of clues. The result of such patient study is a huge body of information—information painstakingly gathered, evaluated, and organized over the years. And it is such information that is vividly capsulized here in ALBUM OF PRE-HISTORIC MAN.

Once again joining forces, author Tom McGowen and artist Rod Ruth bring to life scenes from the ancient past, focusing on our prehuman and human ancestors—from the caterpillar-eating, tree-dwelling creatures of 15 million years ago to the resourceful and inventive humans who learned to make tools, use fire, and farm the land.

ALBUM OF PREHISTORIC MAN presents a fascinating account of human evolution. Fast-moving and up-to-date, this book surveys millions of years of human history with remarkable life, coherence, and brevity.

Album of Prehistoric Man

Revised and Updated Edition

By TOM McGOWEN

Illustrated by ROD RUTH

CHECKERBOARD PRESS

New York

Text and illustrations reviewed and
authenticated by Dr. Glen H. Cole
Curator of Prehistory
Field Museum of Natural History
Chicago, Illinois

Library of Congress Cataloging-in-Publication Data
McGowen, Tom.
    Album of prehistoric man.
    Reprint. Originally published: © 1975.
    Includes index.
    Summary: A brief introduction to the evolution and
characteristics of prehistoric people from apelike
prehumans to modern human beings.
    1. Man, Prehistoric—Juvenile literature.   [1. Man,
Prehistoric.   2. Evolution]   I. Ruth, Rod, ill.
II. Title.
GN744.M38   1987   573.3   87–11630
ISBN 0-02-688514-X

CHECKERBOARD PRESS and colophon are trademarks of Macmillan, Inc.

Contents

Ashes, Bones, and Stone Tools 8

Unknown Ancestors 12

The First Hominids 16

Hominids and First Humans 20

The Upright People 24

The Neanderthal People 28

The Ice Age 32

People Like Us 36

The Cave Artists 40

The Ice Age Americans 44

The Great Change 48

Tombs, Temples, and Standing Stones 52

Metal and Marks in Clay 56

Pronunciation Guide 59

Index 59

Ashes, Bones, and Stone Tools

THE SUN was setting. At the edge of a clump of trees on a rolling plain, a short, thick-bodied man with an apelike face and sloping skull squatted over the carcass of a newly killed deer. With a fist-sized, jaggedly pointed rock, he hacked the skin from the deer's body in several places and peeled it off. Putting down the tool, he helped another man lay the skinned carcass atop a pile of burning twigs and brush.

His mouth watering and his stomach rumbling, the man crouched by the fire in the twilight with the other hunters and the women and children. He sniffed eagerly at the odor of the roasting meat. When it was done, he and the others gobbled down their shares, then stretched out around the fire. With full bellies, they were soon asleep.

At the first light of dawn, the little group of people was on its way again, the hunters searching for signs that would lead them to another day's food. On a platterlike piece of flat stone, one of the women carried some of the still faintly glowing coals. They would be used to start another cooking fire when one was needed. The people left their encampment as it was—a circle of nearly dead fire and a quantity of scattered, charred bones. Also left behind, forgotten by the man who had skinned the deer, was the jagged stone tool.

Half a million years ago, people such as these lived in small bands in many parts of Europe, Africa, and Asia. They were our ancestors—part of the long chain of prehistoric humans and prehumans that stretches down millions of years, and of which we are simply the newest link. Some of the creatures in that chain were little more than apes. Some were no different from modern humans.

How do we know about these prehistoric ancestors of ours? How do we know what they looked like and how they lived? How do we know they even were our ancestors?

The answers to such questions are not simple. All together they make up a kind of detective story—a story of the work of many kinds of scientists during many years.

To begin with, What is a human? That's a question scientists had to answer when they first began studying prehistoric people. For while many kinds of these prehistoric people did not look like modern humans and were not able to do many of the things we can do, they could do things that no ordinary animal can.

To be called *human,* then, a creature has to be a combination of things. A human belongs to the order of animals called *Primates*—the same group that apes and monkeys belong to. A human walks and runs upright, on two legs. Humans live in groups and cooperate with one another. Humans communicate with each other by means of language. A human has a well-developed brain with which it can plan and imagine things and solve difficult problems. And a human has the ability to think up tools for special purposes and the skill to make and use them. Many animals can do some of these things; only a human can do them all.

It was through the detective work of many scientists that we have been able to learn which prehistoric creatures fit the human role. And detective work of this sort is often done with just such evidence as the band of hunters' abandoned campsite of half a million years ago.

Scientists know that after a time, the remains of the fire, the charred bones, and the tool that the man left behind might be covered up by dead leaves and grass, dust, and soil washed over them by rain. After half a million years, they would still be where they were left, only buried many feet deep.

If an anthropologist—a scientist who studies human beings—were to dig down and uncover these things, he would be able to tell a great deal from them. To most anyone else, the stone tool would simply look like a piece of broken rock. But an anthropologist could tell that chips had been knocked off the stone in a certain way. By striking it with another stone, someone had given it a kind of point and cutting edge. No animal could ever have done, nor even thought of, such a thing. It could only have been done by a creature who could imagine in advance what the tool should look like and who had hands skillful enough to chip one stone with another until it looked the way that creature wanted it to. Such evidence would tell the anthropologist that the tool had been made by a human.

The ashes and bits of charcoal would also say *human* to the anthropologist, for humans are the only creatures able to make campfires. As for the bones, they could only have become charred by being in the fire. And the only reason animal bones would have been put into fire would be to cook the meat around them. Additionally, the number of bones and the way they were scattered about would suggest to the anthropologist that a number of people had eaten pieces of the meat.

Weighing all this evidence, the anthropologist would know that a group of creatures who could make tools and use fire had once been here and had cooked and eaten an animal they had probably killed. There could be little doubt they were human.

An important question now would be, When had this happened? The anthropologist would have a number of ways of determining this. One of the best ways makes use of the work of other scientists—physicists and chemists. A small bit of one of the bones is put through a chemical process, and a certain chemical in it is measured. This amount of chemical shows approximately how old the bone is.

The next question would be, What did these humans of half a million years ago look like?

To answer that, an anthropologist needs some of their bones. Even just a few bits and pieces can tell a great deal. From the top part of a skull, for example, it is possible to see how big a brain an animal had. A hipbone shows how a creature walked. From a few teeth, it is possible to tell what group of animals a creature belonged to—apes or bears or elephants or humans. A skull shows what an animal's head looked like, and bones from its body show its shape.

Bones of half-million-year-old humans have been found, together with their tools, remains of their camps, and bones of animals they killed. Their skulls show that they were primates, as are apes and humans, and that they looked much more apelike than we do. But their skulls also show that their brains, although not as large as ours, were much larger than the brains of chimpanzees, the smartest animals next to humans today. So, scientists believe that these half-million-year-old humans must have been much smarter than chimpanzees, though not nearly as smart as we are. Their arm and leg bones show that their bodies were much like ours, only smaller, and their hipbones show that they walked upright, just as we do. And, from the shape of the space in their jaws where the muscles of their tongues and vocal cords were, some scientists think they could speak in a slow, clumsy sort of language.

Thus, from bones, tools, remains of campsites, and remains of food, anthropologists have been able to put together pictures of our prehistoric ancestors—from those that lived many millions of years ago and were simply a smarter kind of animal, to those who were just like humans of today and began our civilization.

But even with such evidence, it's important to remember that we don't know everything, and we're not sure of everything. There are still many gaps and holes in our knowledge of our ancestors, and some of the things we think we know about them are based on nothing more than careful guesses. Sometimes, scientists do not agree on what a tool was used for or on whether a bone is truly human. And sometimes, things we think we knew for sure turn out to be wrong when new discoveries are made.

So, as you read about your prehistoric ancestors, remember that our knowledge of them is still growing and changing. But the story of our ancestors, as far as we have pieced it together—how they made the change from animals to humans, how they used their skills and cunning to survive in a savage world, and how they slowly tamed that world and became its masters—is wonderful and exciting and something we can be proud of. For the story of our prehistoric ancestors is *our* story, too!

Monkey

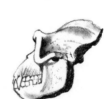

Gorilla

Australopithecus

Neanderthal

Cro-Magnon

Unknown Ancestors

THE BLACK night sky slowly turned gray, announcing the rising of the sun. As the light brightened, it pushed the shadows out from a patch of forest lying along the banks of a stream. In the forest, a creature that was sleeping in the branches of a tree was awakened by the first light that fell upon its closed eyes. Sitting up, the creature yawned a huge yawn, peeling back its lips, showing most of its teeth. It sat for a while, blinking and scratching itself, and then it swiftly clambered down out of the tree and stood on the ground.

The creature was like an ape, and yet not like an ape. There were small differences. It was hairy and had a typical ape head that jutted forward out of its shoulders on a thick neck, but its legs were not as short and bowed as an ape's, and its feet were longer and more narrow than an ape's handlike feet. When it took a few steps, instead of bending over and leaning its weight on its hands as an ape does, this creature walked almost upright with its hands held well off the ground.

Nearby, bushes parted and a creature like the first emerged from the forest. The two looked at one another amiably and then shuffled off together in search of food. They knew each other—they were both members of a little group of these creatures that lived and searched for food together. One after another, the others of the group appeared and spread out, moving leisurely among the trees and peering about at the ground in search of berries, seeds, tender buds and shoots, and perhaps a tasty caterpillar or two....

Creatures such as these may have lived about 15 million years ago on the edge of plains in patches of forest that grew along streams in Africa and India. The creature has been named *Ramapithecus*, "Rama's ape," after the Hindu god Rama.

Only a few fragments of jaw belonging to Ramapithecus have been discovered, and so all that is known about it for sure is that its teeth were much more human than apelike. But this, together with the kind of place it lived in, causes most anthropologists to suspect that Ramapithecus probably spent most of its time on the ground and that it walked nearly upright. At one time, most scientists thought that Ramapithecus belonged to the family of animals known as *hominids*, which is the family *we* belong to, and that it might have been our ancestor. It's now known that isn't correct. However,

12

RAMAPITHECUS

Prosimian

there's no doubt that the ancestor of humans was a creature probably very much like Ramapithecus—an apelike creature.

It's not surprising that one of our ancestors looked like an ape, because apes and humans are cousins. We both had the same ancestor. Both of our families belong to the order of primates—the same group that monkeys, lemurs, tarsiers, and a number of other tree-dwelling creatures belong to. And to understand how our apelike ancestors came to be, we have to go back to the primates' beginnings, about 65 million years ago.

At that time, a number of little, ratlike animals were scurrying and scampering about in the underbrush and shrubbery of tropical forests. These animals are called *prosimians*, meaning "before monkeys," and they were the ancestors of all the primates—humans included.

It seems incredible that these long-tailed, sharp-nosed, mouse-sized little beasts could have been the roots of our family tree, but they were. Sixty-five million years of evolution—the natural force whereby animals slowly and continuously change during millions of years—shaped some of the descendants of the prosimians into us.

Evolution takes place within a group of animals called a *species*—animals that are all of the same kind and that can mate and have babies. (Animals that are of different species, such as dogs and cats, cannot mate with each other.) And it is by means of the babies born within a species, generation after generation, that evolution takes place.

In every generation of animals in a spe-

cies, there are many differences. Some animals will be big, some small. Some will be quicker than others, some a little differently colored, and so on. And some of these differences may help a young animal survive while most of its brothers and sisters are getting killed and eaten! Thus, animals that have differences which help them get more food or help them to protect themselves are more likely to grow up to mate and have babies. And they will pass their helpful differences on to some of their babies—who in turn will have a better chance of growing up and passing along the differences they inherited. After a long while, most of the animals in a species will be descendants of those animals that had helpful or useful differences. And by that time, they may have changed so much and in so many ways, that they scarcely resemble their ancestors.

In this way, through evolution, some of the descendants of the early prosimians changed. Some anthropologists and other scientists think that the earliest prosimians were ratlike creatures that hunted insects among the bushes and lower tree branches of forests. Instead of having widely spread eyes, like those of squirrels and rabbits, these creatures may have had eyes that were closer together, like the eyes of a cat. Additionally, they may have had rather handlike paws with which they seized the insects they stalked. Gradually, some of them may have moved higher into the trees. Their handlike paws were helpful there, enabling them to grasp branches. And their closely set eyes, which saw things in depth (as we do, instead of in flat images like pictures in a book as

Lemur

Gibbon

Aegyptopithecus

most animals see them), were very useful in judging distances among the tangled zigzag of branches. Through the years, the animals with the best vision and most handlike paws were probably those that survived best and passed along their traits. Slowly, then, through the process of evolution, the eyesight of their descendants improved, and they became cleverer with their hands. Also as they evolved, their snouts shortened, enabling them to see better, and the size of their brains increased, making them smarter.

In this way, the descendants of the prosimians grew more and more monkeylike and apelike. By about 30 million years ago, some of them had made the change. At about that time, in a thick, green forest in Egypt, now a desert, there lived a creature that has been named *Aegyptopithecus*, meaning "Egypt ape." It was about 3 feet long, with a tail and a still rather long snout, but it was very apelike, and scientists think it probably was the ancestor of all apelike creatures—Ramapithecus, orangutans, gibbons, chimpanzees, gorillas, and hominids.

So the process of evolution, through which the descendants of the prosimians changed into many kinds of primates, may have caused some of Aegyptopithecus's descendants to develop in several different directions. For a long time, these descendants, like Aegyptopithecus, continued to live in trees. And if they ventured down onto the ground, they moved on all fours, leaning forward and resting the weight of their upper bodies on their arms.

But some of these creatures began to spend more and more time on the ground. Scientists believe that somewhere between 7 to 10 million years ago, these creatures split into two different groups. One group included the creatures that were the ancestors of gorillas and chimpanzees. The others were the ancestors of humans. In this group, hind feet slowly evolved from handlike members for grasping branches into humanlike feet for supporting the weight of the body. As their legs lengthened, the creatures became more able at walking upright without putting their hands on the ground. Thus, their hands became free to hold things. They probably slept in trees at night, but by day they moved about on the ground, seeking seeds and leafy plants, as well as berries, insects, and even small amounts of meat from dead animals. These apelike creatures that had begun to walk nearly upright were the first true hominids.

Chimpanzee

Gorilla

Early Hominid

The First Hominids

THUNDER CRASHED and lightning flared in a dark gray sky above a broad plain beside a small lake. The plain was in what would one day be the country of Ethiopia, in Africa. There was a patter of raindrops, then the sky opened and a flood of rain came driving down.

A number of creatures were making their way along a dry riverbed that ran through the plain. They were furry and apelike, with small heads and long arms, and most of them were no more than 4 feet tall. But they did not walk as apes do, bent over and with the knuckles of the hands touching the ground. These creatures walked with bent legs, their bodies slouched forward; their arms swung at their sides. They did not have the handlike feet of an ape, with widespread toes; their feet were more human in shape.

There were thirteen of them, nine adults and four young ones. They whimpered as the driving rain pelted them, and cringed each time there was an explosion of thunder. They were heading toward a thick grove of trees where they sometimes took shelter, and where they could huddle together for comfort until the rain ended.

But they had made a serious mistake in using the dry riverbed—with its high banks rising on each side—as the route to their shelter. For as the rain continued to pour down, tons of water were beginning to run from the highest parts of the land toward the lowest—and the riverbed was one of the lowest. Water was soon pouring into it from numerous streams coursing down from high ground. A flash flood was building up!

The apelike creatures splashed along in water up to their ankles, their animal brains unable to comprehend the danger that was fast closing in on them. Only as the water swirled around their knees did they begin to realize they were in trouble. With shrieks of fear, they tried to scramble up the banks.

But it was too late. Water now raced through the riverbed in a torrent, and the little creatures were quickly swept away in the swelling flood. Helplessly threshing and floundering, the creatures drowned, and their bodies were carried along by the rushing water.

The rain slackened and soon stopped. The runoff from the high ground shrank to a trickle. The speed of the flooded stream slowed down. In time the drifting bodies of the dead apelike creatures arrived at a bend in the river, where they began to pile up

First Hominids

Homo Habilis

Homo Erectus

Homo Sapiens
Neanderthalensis

Homo Sapiens Sapiens (Cro-Magnon)

against the muddy bank. Gradually they were covered by the mud that was carried to the river bend by the flowing water.

The sun came out again, and life resumed in the land by the lake. There were hundreds of prowling creatures that would have gladly feasted on the bodies of the dead apelike things, dragging them off and scattering their bones, but because they were buried under mud they were not found by any of the carrion eaters. The sun soon baked the mud into clay.

Years passed. There were scores of other flash floods, and the layer of mud over the buried apelike creatures grew higher each time. The mud became clay, and over a long period of time the clay was compressed into stone. The soft parts of the apelike creatures had long since decomposed, but their bones still lay jumbled together, embedded in the stone.

Millions of years went by. And some 3 million years after the apelike creatures had met their deaths in the flash flood, scientists digging in the rock that had been the riverbank discovered their bones.

The bones of these thirteen creatures, apparently victims of a flash flood (it is not certain that they did, indeed, die that way), were not the first remains of such 3-million-year-old apelike creatures to have been discovered. Scientists working in Ethiopia some time earlier had found an apelike knee bone. A little later, part of a jaw was unearthed. Then, in 1974, nearly all of an entire skeleton was discovered. It was the skeleton of a 3-foot-tall female, and the scientists who found it nicknamed it "Lucy."

The discovery of "Lucy" and the thirteen others, as well as additional pieces of creatures that had lived in the land of the lake, were major events for scientists who were trying to piece together the history of the human race. For it was obvious from the shapes of the bones of these creatures—of their hip, leg, and foot bones—that they had apparently walked upright, much as humans do. Their teeth were also much more like human teeth than ape teeth. Altogether, they seemed more humanlike than apelike, and this meant they were probably hominids: members of the same family of creatures to which humans belong. They were the oldest hominids that had ever been discovered.

But although they seemed to be hominids, it was obvious they were not humans. Their brains were still much too small and apelike, and certain other parts of their bodies were more like those of an ape than a human. So the scientists who had discovered them gave them the name *Australopithecus afarensis*, meaning "southern ape of the Afar region" (a part of Ethiopia). It was the belief of these scientists that the creatures were probably the ancestors of all other hominids—which would mean, of course, that they were *our* ancestors.

However, as is usually the case, many other scientists do not agree with this at all. For one thing, there are apparently differences between the skeletons of some of these creatures. The skeleton of "Lucy," for example, is much smaller than the skeletons of any of the nine adults of the group of thirteen that was found all together. Some scientists think this means that "Lucy" was actually a completely different kind of creature. And if "Lucy" was different—if there were actually two different kinds of hominids living in the land by the lake—then probably neither of them was really the first hominid. Instead, they were probably both just descendants of whatever creature *was* the first true hominid.

Some scientists do not even think "Lucy" and the other creatures were hominids at all. They believe that the creatures were just a kind of ape that probably really couldn't walk upright very well.

But many scientists feel certain that "Lucy" and the others were all the same species, or kind, of creature—all *Australopithecus afarensis*—and that they were true hominids, probably the very first kind of hominid. They think *Australopithecus afarensis* was the ancestor of several different kinds of hominids that lived in Africa much later. They believe it may even have been the ancestor of the first true human, *Homo habilis*, as well as all the other humans that came

after—*Homo erectus, Homo Neanderthal,* and the people known as Cro-Magnons, who were the first of *our* kind of human.

Australopithecus afarensis is a subject of great argument among scientists. All that we know for sure about these creatures is that they were from 3 to 4 feet tall, they were sturdy and strong, they probably walked upright in some manner, and while they had very apelike skulls and brains about the size of a chimpanzee's brain, they had human-like teeth and feet. They lived in open, grassy plains dotted with clumps of trees, and ate plants, insects, bird and reptile eggs, and probably small amounts of meat from dead animals they found. It does not appear that they knew how to break stones in order to make cutting tools, for no such broken stones have been found among any of their remains.

Were they just a kind of ape? Or were they, indeed, the first hominids and the ancestors of the human race? No one can yet say for sure.

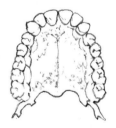

Teeth of Ape   Teeth of Human

Hominids and First Humans

BENEATH A PAIR of brooding volcanoes that thrust their great cones up among the clouds lay a small lake. The shallow water at one end was a mass of pink and scarlet bodies—a huge flock of stilt-legged flamingos feeding. Nearby, on the wooded shore, a herd of big, gray elephantlike beasts was browsing. A lone rhinoceros clumped down to the water's edge, ignored by—and ignoring—the flamingos. He noisily gulped his fill, then turned and trotted out onto the broad plain that spread away from the lake.

The rhino thudded past a troop of foraging baboons and a herd of grazing zebras. He passed within 50 feet of a big saber-toothed cat lying hidden among some bushes and trotted on toward a distant patch of trees. As he skirted this little woods, a large, apelike creature emerged from among the trees.

The creature stood blinking in the full sunlight that bathed the plain. A full-grown male, he was about 5 feet tall, with a powerful, thickly muscled body that probably weighed as much as 150 pounds. He looked much like a gorilla, but there was one enormous difference. Gorillas stand and walk bent over, with the knuckles of their hands pressed against the ground. And so they are

four-footed animals. But this creature stood upright, and when he moved, he walked on two legs, in short, plodding steps, his hands hanging at his sides.

He stopped beside a tree, one hand resting on the trunk, and stared out across the plain. A small fruit hanging from a low branch caught his eye, and solemnly he plucked it and popped it into his mouth. Behind him, a small group of similar creatures moved slowly out of the trees, carefully examining the ground and the low branches of the trees as they approached.

The big male and these others had been feeding in this patch of woods for several days and had just about stripped it bare of their kind of food. But now, the big male was eyeing another wooded patch visible half a mile away on the plain. Dimly he was aware that food might be plentiful there, and abruptly he started in that direction. Another male hurried to join him, and the others quickly streamed after.

The group of creatures kept close to one another, for there was danger on the plain from several kinds of prowling flesh eaters. If the band encountered a lion or saber-toothed cat, the big male and the other males would probably have tried to scare it

Flamingos

Rhinoceros

20

Zebras

Australopithecus

off by showing their teeth and making noise.

Halfway to the new patch of forest, there was a rise in the ground. The big male, followed by the others, plodded flat-footedly to its top. Once there, he stopped dead in his tracks. Below, on the descending slope, was another group of creatures.

These, too, were apelike, and they walked upright on two legs. But they were different. They were smaller—approximately 4½ feet tall, and slim and wiry rather than thickly muscled. Their faces were a little less apelike than those of the bigger creatures. Most of them carried things in their hands—pieces of sharp-edged broken bones and rocks. One of them carried a small, ratlike dead animal, its fur matted with blood.

The two groups stared at one another. The big male's eyes caught the eyes of one of the smaller creatures, also a male, and for just a moment there was tension. Then, as if to show a lack of interest, the big male averted his gaze, as did all the others. Slowly, the group of smaller creatures turned aside and began to drift off through the grass, eyes down, concentrating pointedly on the search for food. The bigger creatures continued on toward the woods, but the big male took a curving detour that got them quickly away from the others. Deliberately paying no attention to one another, the two groups moved apart....

Such an encounter might well have taken place in eastern Africa some 2 million years ago. For scientists think there may have been as many as four different kinds of hominids living there at that time, all probably descended from *Australopithecus afarensis*. Dif-

ferent groups of these creatures must have sometimes encountered one another.

Three kinds of these creatures also have the name *Australopithecus: Australopithecus africanus* ("southern ape of Africa"), *Australopithecus robustus* ("sturdy southern ape"), and *Australopithecus boisei*, named for a scientist. Although their name means "ape," they were even less apelike than *Australopithecus afarensis* had been. They walked and ran upright, which no ape can do for very long, and their teeth and brains were much more humanlike than apelike.

The big *Australopithecus robustus* was most like an ape. It was probably a mild-mannered eater of plants, much like a gorilla, feeding on tender shoots, juicy leaves, roots, fruit, seeds, and nuts. But it may well have eaten small animals, too, if it had the chance. It probably used tools, such as sticks for digging and stones for pounding.

Australopithecus boisei was probably much like *robustus*. A sturdily built 5-footer, it had wide cheekbones, a flat face, and such big, powerful-looking teeth that newspaper reporters nicknamed it "Nutcracker man" when they first saw its skull. It did, indeed, seem as if *boisei* could have cracked nutshells with such teeth.

The third kind of *Australopithecus* was quite different. These creatures were smaller—about 4½ feet tall—and slim and wiry rather than thickly muscled. Their faces were a little less apelike. They were probably a good deal less fussy about their food than the bigger hominids. They scrounged for whatever they could find as they moved slowly through the knee-deep grass of the

22

plains where they lived, peering about for seeds, berries, tasty roots, insects, caterpillars, bird eggs, turtles, and most anything else. With luck, they might have found a helpless baby antelope or gazelle hiding in the grass, which they could bash in the head with a rock. Or they might have caught and killed a young baboon that strayed away from its herd. Sometimes they found left-over meat from the kill of a lion or saber-toothed cat, but they probably had to fight off hyenas and vultures to get a share. And often, one of *them* became a hunting beast's prey.

While there is a possibility that these smaller *Australopithecus africanuses* were the ancestors of true humans, most scientists think not. They think that all three kinds of *Australopithecus* just died out, in time, and the *Australopithecus* line became extinct, probably about a million years ago.

But the other kind of hominid living in Africa at the same time as the Australopithecines survived, and may have been the ancestor of every person living today. Most scientists think it was the first human. It is called *Homo habilis*, or "skillful man."

Homo habilis lived in eastern Africa about 2 million years ago. It was about 5 feet tall, sturdier than *Australopithecus africanus*, but not as muscular as either *robustus* or *boisei*. It had a bigger brain than any of those three creatures, and its face was not as apelike as theirs. Its teeth, hands, and feet were much more like those of humans of today.

Homo habilis had a very different way of life from the Australopithecines. It was a tool-maker and hunter. By pounding one rock with another to knock off chips and form a sharp cutting edge, these early humans produced the world's first *manufactured* tool—a crude sort of chopper and slicer that could also be used as an ax to smash into an animal's skull. *Homo habilis* may have hunted baboons, for many crushed baboon skulls have been found where *habilis* lived. Animal bones with cut marks, where meat was sliced from the bone, have also been found. *Homo habilis* probably lived in little groups, and the males did the hunting while the females and children moved through the tall grass of tree-dotted plains, gathering seeds, fruit, insects, and eggs. At night, the members of the group probably slept in trees for safety.

Homo habilis may have been descended from *Australopithecus afarensis*, or from some other early hominid we don't yet know about. But *habilis* almost certainly was the ancestor of the next kind of human, which spread out into the world, learned to use fire, and hunted the very largest animals.

Australopithecus

Baboons

23

The Upright People

IN A BROAD and grassy valley between tall cliffs, a small group of elephants was feeding. They were huge creatures, 13 feet high, with incredible 10-foot-long tusks that jutted straight out like immense spears. The big, gray beasts moved slowly, with ponderous unconcern, as if aware that their size, bulk, and terrible tusks made them nearly invincible. Not even the big, ferocious saber-toothed cats that prowled this prehistoric world would dare attack a whole group of these giants—nor, probably, even a single full-grown one.

But, there was one kind of creature that was willing to venture such an attack. A pair of eager, cunning eyes was watching the elephants as they slowly moved deeper into the valley. They were the eyes of a man.

He was a rather short man, a little more than 5 feet tall, with a thick, heavy-muscled body. His head was somewhat apelike —he had a low forehead that sloped back, a flattened nose, a big, pushed-out mouth, and practically no chin. A wooden spear was clutched in his fist, and lying beside him was a flat slab of stone on which a small pile of coals glinted. From time to time, the man bent forward to blow on the coals, fanning them into a red glow.

He was not alone. A number of other men lay hidden among the rocks at the bottom of the cliffs. All of them had been awaiting the coming of the elephants and were now ready to act according to plan.

When the elephants had made their way sufficiently far into the valley, the man picked up the slab with his free hand and stole cautiously out of hiding. The others followed. They fanned out in a broad semi-circle. A steady wind, perfect for their purpose, blew into the valley. The man blew fiercely onto his pile of coals then dumped them onto the dry, autumn grass. Several other men, also carrying coals, did the same.

Fanned by the brisk wind, the grass caught fire almost instantly. The man crouched back, ready to flee if the fire did not move in the proper direction. But the blaze quickly spread and began to move away from him and the others, into the valley, sending spirals of acrid, blue smoke swirling before it.

The tips of the elephants' trunks began to twitch as the sharp tang of the smoke reached them. They halted their feeding and began to stamp and rumble, nervously staring about. Several of them caught sight

24

HOMO ERECTUS

Elephants

of the flickering line of brightness rolling toward them through the grass, and instantly, they panicked. Trumpeting with terror, they broke into lumbering strides, fleeing from the thing they feared most. The other elephants thudded behind.

Near the center of the valley there were several large patches of bog—oozy mud, many feet deep and thick as glue. Most of the elephants thundered past these mud traps, but five of the animals—three adults and two half-grown ones—blundered straight into one of the bogs. In seconds, they were floundering belly-deep in the soft, clinging slime, unable to move.

When the fire burned itself out, the man and his fellow hunters rushed at their helpless prey. With their lighter bodies, the men could wade into the mud to attack the trapped beasts. The elephants wallowed and trumpeted in terror and fury as the men, avoiding the dangerous trunks and tusks, stabbed and stabbed with their spears and hurled big, jagged rocks at the animals' heads.

It took a long time to stab and batter the elephants until they weakened and died from loss of blood, but finally the slaughter was finished. Now there was meat—plenty of meat—to be hacked off the carcasses and divided up among the hunters. This day, they and their women and children would feast!

A hunt such as this actually took place in a valley in Spain about 300 thousand years ago. Scientists have found the bones of the slaughtered elephants, the tools the hunters used to cut them up, and traces of the fire that apparently was set. These skillful, cunning hunters, brave enough to tackle the biggest of all beasts, were the descendants of the australopithecines. But they were humans.

The change from Australopithecus to human probably took place between 1 and 1½ million years ago. By about 800 thousand years ago, the human descendants of the australopithecines were moving out of their tropical and subtropical homeland into the cooler, more northern sections of Asia and Europe. These people have been named *Homo erectus,* meaning "upright man." They walked exactly the way we do and had bodies much like ours, except that they were shorter and stockier and had thicker bones, and heads that were still somewhat apelike. Were they hairy? Probably not— at least no more so than many people living now. However, even though they were like us in some ways, their brains were much smaller, and they were a long, long way from being as intelligent.

But they were far more intelligent and skillful than their australopithecine ancestors. As time went on, they created more kinds of more efficient tools. They learned to chip pieces of flint all over, flattening them out and giving them points and edges for chopping and cutting. They also made a kind of tool that could have been used for scraping all the shreds of meat and fat off the insides of the skins of animals they killed. This could mean that they may have used animal skins for some kind of clothing —perhaps draping them about their shoulders like cloaks. Or, they could have used

skins as bags to carry things in.

In addition, the Homo erectus people were the first creatures in the world to use fire. They probably could not actually make blazes of their own, but they may have picked up burning branches from forest fires started by lightning or volcanic eruptions and used these to start campfires. Once they had a fire going in some protected place, they had only to keep it fed with dry leaves, grass, and twigs. At a cave in China used by Homo erectus people as a shelter for hundreds of years, scientists found the remains of a fire that may have been kept going in this manner for many generations. The ashes were 20 feet deep.

Fire was an extremely important tool for the Homo erectus people, just as it has been for all humans since. It kept them warm, and it kept dangerous animals away from their shelters. They learned to cook meat in fire, making it tastier and much easier to chew. They also apparently discovered that putting green wood among the coals of a fire would harden and toughen the wood before it began to burn, for they used fire to harden the points of their wooden spears.

Although the Homo erectus people sometimes used caves as shelters, they weren't cavemen. Apparently, they more often built shelters out of tree branches. With their chopping tools, they hacked branches from young trees, probably trimming off the twigs, and then they poked the branches into the ground in a rough circle, holding them in place by piling rocks against them. The tops of the branches were probably bent and twisted together so that the finished hut was more or less tent shaped. The remains of such a hut have been found—holes made by branches that were pushed into the ground, rocks that were once piled against these branches, and a circle of stones in the center where a fire was kept burning.

But although these people could build crude huts, they did not live together in villages. They were nomads—hunters who lived in small bands, roaming from place to place in search of animals they could kill for food. The kinds of animals they hunted depended upon where the nomads lived, but their menu included deer, horse, bear, water buffalo, camel, boar, baboon, cat, fox, rhinoceros, and elephant. They also ate many kinds of plant food.

To hunt such a variety of animals, often using fire and traps, the Homo erectus hunters must have had some way of making plans and communicating ideas to each other. Thus, some scientists think the Homo erectus people may have been able to talk. But if they had a language, it was probably crude and slow, and made up of a small number of words that had to be helped out with gestures.

The Homo erectus people lived from about 1⅓ million years ago to about 200 thousand years ago in little bands scattered throughout Africa, Asia, and Europe. Their faces were apelike and their ways were crude, but they were definitely a species, or kind, of human being, and the ancestors of the first of *our* kind of human being.

The Neanderthal People

THE SKY was a mass of sullen, gray clouds that blotted out the sun's face. A chilly wind swept through the valley, bringing a swirl of cold rain that spattered into the river and pelted against the limestone cliffs that rose above it.

At intervals in the long face of the cliff there were dark dots of cave mouths, and in one of these, an orange light flickered. A man was standing just inside the cave entrance. He was thickset and muscular, and he held high a flaring pine branch. The light from this torch glowed upon a trio of other men who were scooping out a long, shallow pit in the cave floor. Their shadows danced on the limestone wall and across the faces of a little cluster of men and women. Against the other wall lay a silent, unmoving shape.

After a time, the three men finished their task. Two of them stepped to the wall and bent to lift the form that lay there. It was the body of a young man.

Gently, they lowered the limp form into the shallow grave. They arranged the dead man so that he lay on his right side, his head pillowed on a mound of flint chips, his right hand tucked beneath his cheek as if he were asleep. Into the grave they put such things as might be needed for a long journey—well-made flint tools and weapons, and chunks of roasted meat. . . .

The young man, buried in that cave overlooking a river near where a little French town sits today, died 50 or 60 thousand years ago. He was only about 16 years old, and the cause of his death is not known. It could have been disease. He was one of the prehistoric people we call *Neanderthals,* so named because their remains were first found in the *Neander thal* ("Neander valley") of Germany.

The Neanderthal people lived across a period of some 60 thousand years, from about 100 thousand to 40 thousand years ago. They were descendants of a little-known people who were apparently descendants of the Homo erectus people. Neanderthal tools and remains have been found in many parts of Europe, central Asia, North Africa, the Near East, and Indonesia.

For a long time, it was thought that Neanderthals must have been crude, hulking, misshapen creatures with ugly, nonhuman faces. The first few Neanderthal skulls found—all in Europe—had foreheads that sloped back, great ridges of bone over the

28

eyes, and hardly any chins. The skeleton of one rather old Neanderthal man seemed to show that these people had walked bent over, with bowed legs. It hardly seemed possible that such creatures could have been related to us, so most scientists thought they were probably an apelike, subhuman race that had simply died out—that had, in fact, probably been killed off by *true* humans.

But then, new finds were made in other parts of the world. Skulls of Neanderthals who did not seem very different from us were discovered, as well as bones that clearly showed that these Neanderthals had walked upright just as we do.

Scientists were puzzled. How could the European Neanderthals have been so different from their relatives in other places? Some scientists took another, closer look at the skeleton of the old, European Neanderthal man and discovered something that earlier scientists examining the skeleton had dismissed. The man had walked bent over and bowlegged only because he had been crippled by arthritis, a disease that still bothers many people today. And it began to seem that perhaps the European Neanderthals had looked a little different from the others because they had lived under completely different conditions. Perhaps the eternal cold, ice, and snow that covered Europe during the thousands of years of the Ice Age had caused them to develop in a way that protected them against the cold. Perhaps their squat bodies, rather ugly by our standards but good for holding in heat, actually helped them to survive.

It now seems clear that the Neanderthals were not a different, subhuman race at all, but were actually members of our own species of the human race, *Homo sapiens*, or "wise man." In fact, it is possible that many people living today may have Neanderthal ancestors.

In general, Neanderthals were a stocky people, muscular and barrel-chested. They ranged from 5 to 5½ feet tall in Europe, and a little taller in other parts of the world. Their fingers and toes seem to have been short and stubby, and their faces tended to be rather large and rugged, with biggish noses and mouths and thick eyebrow ridges. But many Neanderthals probably did not look very different from some people of today.

The Neanderthals had a greater variety of tools than their ancestors. Instead of merely knocking chips off a piece of flint until they had a chopper or hand ax, the Neanderthals learned how to strike differently shaped chips from a chunk of flint and then shape the chips into many different kinds of tools—points, knives, scrapers, borers, spear sharpeners. The number of flint scrapers made by Neanderthals seems to show that they cleaned animal skins, which they then probably used to make clothing. Another tool, a kind of punch, may have been used for poking holes into skins. This could mean that Neanderthal clothing was held together with strips of animal skin laced through holes. Still another tool was a flake of flint with a curved notch in it. This was probably used for shaping and sharpening long branches into spears, which were then hardened in hot coals.

Cleaning Animal Skin

30

Among the many tools and weapons that have been found at Neanderthal caves and campsites are some things of no usefulness at all. They are simply pretty. One Neanderthal cut a bit of elephant tooth into an egg-shape, then carefully smoothed and polished it. Another of these people apparently collected pretty stones and shells—a piece of shiny fool's gold, a fossil seashell, a round chunk of coral. A person of today would collect such things because they are attractive and interesting. Is this why the Neanderthal kept them? If so, it could mean that the Neanderthals had an appreciation of beauty, just as we do. Of course, this isn't surprising if they actually were the first of our kind of people.

Another thing that makes the Neanderthals seem more like us than any of the people who came before them is the way they treated their dead. Unlike the earlier prehistoric people who simply let their dead lie, some of the Neanderthals buried those that died. In some cases, stone tools, animal bones and other things were put into the graves with the dead people. One grave has been found in which the dead person was placed on a bed of pine branches and then covered with flowers, which certainly seems to show that the Neanderthals had special ceremonies for burying their dead. Perhaps they even believed that the dead ones would come to life again in another world where they would need food and tools. Customs like these may have been part of a kind of religion—perhaps the first religion in the world.

Another evidence of a religious or magical ceremony was found in a high mountain cave near the Swiss-Austrian border. Scientists found a kind of chest made of slabs of rock piled together. Inside this stone box were the skulls of seven huge cave bears. They had been carefully arranged, with their snouts pointing toward the cave entrance, and in front of the box were the remains of many fires. Apparently, when the Neanderthal hunters of this area killed a bear, they cut off its head and put it into the box. Was this supposed to be an act of magic to help the men have successful hunts? Was it a way of keeping the bears' ghosts from haunting the hunters?

The Neanderthal people seem to have disappeared suddenly, about 40 thousand years ago, at the time new people exactly like *us* appeared. Scientists wonder what happened to the Neanderthals and where the new people came from. Did the new people kill off the Neanderthals? Did the Neanderthals and new people live together and create a single race? Or did the Neanderthals simply evolve, or change into, the new people? No one is sure.

The Ice Age

THE CAVE was filled with smoke, smells, and shadows. Around an open fire crackling noisily on the dirt floor sat a number of people busy at tasks. With a pointed stone tool, a woman worked holes into a half-finished leather garment, while two other women vigorously chewed animal skins to make them soft and pliant. A fourth woman nursed a baby, and a gray-haired man with a twisted, withered arm was sorting bones and chunks of flint into piles. Both the women and the man were dressed in roughly made, Eskimo-like fur clothing.

At the cave's entrance, several long, trimmed branches had been driven upright into the ground, with several other branches lashed to them crosswise. On this frame hung a number of animal skins, all laced together to form a kind of curtain that screened out cold wind and helped hold in some of the fire's warmth.

The woman who had been using the stone tool put down her work and rose to her feet. Moving to the entrance, she pushed aside an edge of the curtain and peered out. The scene that met her eyes was bleak. The cave overlooked a snow-covered valley. The sky was lead-gray. In the distance, a cluster of reddish-brown shapes moved against a

background of a shaggy green line of pine trees, and a faint trumpeting reached the woman's ears. Mammoths. And far in the distance, barely visible, what looked like a grayish-white band of low-lying clouds stretched across the horizon. It was the edge of a gigantic sheet of ice which had spread out from mountains well beyond the ice front. The woman couldn't know that there was, far to the north, a much larger sheet of ice more than a mile thick and thousands of miles wide.

But the view did not seem unusual to the woman—she had seen it every day of her life. As far as she knew, this was the way things always had been and always would be. She peered out a while longer, squinting at the uninterrupted white of the landscape, searching for the moving specks that would be the men returning from their hunt. But she could see no sign of them. She turned back into the cave to continue to work and wait beside the life-sustaining fire.

For many of our prehistoric ancestors, just as it was for that woman, the world was a place of long, bitter winters. In Europe, parts of Asia, and North America, generation after generation of humans spent much of their lives in constant battle against snow,

Glacier

ice, and cold. For these people lived during the glacial periods of the Ice Age, when many parts of the world were covered by enormous sheets of ice.

The Ice Age seems to have begun about 1,200,000 years ago. Exactly what happened, and why, we do not know—but the earth's climate grew cooler. Then, as now, great masses of snow often lay in hollows on mountain slopes. In summer, the heat of the sun melted tons of snow off each mountain every day. The water coursed down the sides of the mountains in swift-moving streams that joined together to form rivers. And the rivers flowed out through valleys, winding their way to the sea. Thus, in summer, the great snowcaps on the mountains slowly shrank. In the winter, fed by snowstorms, they grew again.

But when the climate became cooler, the snowstorms began earlier and went on until much later in the spring. The great snow piles did not shrink as much during the shorter, cooler summers, and they grew even larger during the longer winters. As many years passed, they became enormous —mountains of snow lying upon mountains of stone.

At the bottom of these immense, cold piles, the snow changed into gritty pebbles of ice. And the titanic weight of the tons of snow piled upon these ice pebbles began to squeeze the ice outward, like jelly might be squeezed out from between two slices of bread by pressing on the top slice. Great fingers of gritty ice flowed out from the enormous piles of snow. Some of them were pushed all the way out of the hollows and

down the mountain slopes.

The downward pull of gravity, and the push of the ice being squeezed out of the snow piles behind them, sent these gritty fingers creeping down the mountainsides. They became broad, thick rivers of flowing ice. Moving only a few feet or less each day, they crept down the mountains and began to inch across the land. Slowly, some of them flowed together, forming gigantic masses of ice that spread out to cover hundreds of thousands of miles of land in northern Europe, Greenland, most of North America, and parts of Asia, South America, and New Zealand.

The lands near these great ice sheets became much like the Arctic region is today. At the edge of the ice, the ground was a frozen tundra on which, during a short, cool "summer" each year, a few kinds of hardy plants were able to grow—mosses, lichens, stunted willow and birch trees only a few feet tall, and some small, flowering plants. Farther from the ice, the tundra gradually changed into grassy plains where purple heather flowered, and where a few juniper trees and dwarf pines grew. Farther still, the plains gave way to slightly warmer, wetter land where immense forests of shaggy pine trees flourished. The animals that roamed the lands near these great ice sheets included the great fur-covered mammoths, rhinoceroses with woolly coats, cave bears, wolves, musk-oxen, and herds of reindeer.

The ice sheets lay upon the land for thousands of years. Then, again, there was a change in the world's climate. Warmer weather returned, and the huge, gray giants

Cave Bear

Reindeer

Wolf

Musk Ox

34

began to melt. Slowly, during many centuries, they shrank back into the places from which they had come.

Behind them, they left changed lands. Their steady, ponderous movement as they pushed forward had gouged out valleys and dug great holes. As the ice melted, water filled up these holes, creating lakes and ponds. In some places, the ice had scraped the land clean, leaving only bare rock. But in other places, it left behind rich, fertile soil that it had scraped up and carried along as it advanced.

In Europe, northern Asia, and North America, the ice sheets moved back into the far north. Along their edges appeared new tundra and grasslands, followed by pine forests. The mammoths and other creatures that were used to a cold environment moved into these far northern lands. Farther south, where the pine forests had been, forests of leafy trees took their place, and animals from warmer, southern lands moved in. Elephants, hippopotamuses, and other animals that are now found only in Africa or Asia roamed countrysides that would become France, Germany, and England.

But the ice sheets were not to remain in the far north. After many thousands of years, the climate once again grew cool, and again, the great rivers of gray ice came ponderously creeping down out of the mountains.

This advance, retreat, and advance of the ice happened many times during the last million and a half years—perhaps as many as 20 times. This is why that period of time is known as the Ice Age. And it was against the background of the Ice Age that many of our prehistoric ancestors of Europe and northern Asia lived. At times, for thousands of years, Neanderthals and the people who came after them lived in a moderate climate with relatively warm summers and relatively mild winters—but for other thousands of years, they lived in the year-round cold that hung over the edges of the great ice sheets.

The last retreat of the ice sheets began about 15 thousand years ago. But was it the *last* retreat? Many scientists think not. They believe that, even now, we are simply living in one of the warm periods between times of cold. If that is so, then sometime in the future, thousands—or perhaps even only hundreds of years from now—the ice sheets will come forth again! Then, humans will once more experience the fury of the Ice Age, just as our prehistoric ancestors did.

People Like Us

IN THE SHADOW of an overhanging cliff near a tentlike shelter made of animal skins, a man and a boy sat cross-legged, their knees nearly touching. In his lap, the man held a large chunk of dark gray flint that he was carefully examining.

The boy scratched his shoulder and gazed absently about at the activity in the camp. Two of the younger children had just brought loads of brush and twigs for the fire, and a man was squatting over a tiny pile of leaves, kindling a blaze. Nearby, another man had just finished cutting the skin from the body of a reindeer that had been killed earlier. The man handed the skin to two young girls who spread it out on the ground, fur side down, and drove small, sharp pieces of bone through its edges to hold it firm. They then began to scrape it clean with sharp-edged stone tools. Their necklaces of animal teeth rattled and swung with the vigor of their movements.

A word from the man brought the boy's attention back to his duties. The man placed the chunk of flint on the ground, then reached down by his side and picked up a length of pointed bone and a round, fist-sized rock. With a few words, he handed these to the boy.

The boy took them, nervously licking his lips. A skilled flintworker could strike dozens of neat, long, slim blades from a chunk such as this. But up until now, whenever the boy had been permitted to try his hand, he had produced only useless chips. However . . .

He eyed the chunk for a few moments and carefully selected his spot. Holding the pointed bone like a chisel, he set its point against the edge of the chunk. Then, with the round rock, he gave the top of the bone a single, sharp blow. A long, thin shard of flint flaked off the chunk and plopped onto the grass.

The man picked it up and examined it while the boy eyed him hopefully. The piece of flint was like the blade of a knife. Its edges were as sharp as broken glass. The man looked up at the boy and grinned, and the youngster flushed with pride. He had done it! He had struck off a piece of stone that could be made into a proper tool. Now he felt sure that someday he would be as good a flintworker as this man who was his teacher!

Thirty thousand years ago, people such as the boy, the flintworker, and the others at the camp beneath the cliff were living in

36

Flakes of Flint

CRO-MAGNON PEOPLE

France and many other parts of Europe. They are the people we call *Cro-Magnons* after the place in France where some of their skeletons and tools were first found. People much like them were living in parts of Africa and Asia.

The Cro-Magnons were descendants of the Neanderthals. But unlike the Neanderthals with their short bodies and somewhat sloping foreheads and pushed-in chins, the Cro-Magnons looked just like us. They ranged from 5 feet, 8 inches to more than 6 feet tall, and they had high foreheads and prominent chins. These people were the first modern humans. In other words, they were not simply *like* us—they *were* us. If a Cro-Magnon baby of 30 thousand years ago could grow up in the world today, it would probably be just as smart and just as able to talk and do things as any of us.

What was the prehistoric world like for these people who were just like us? It was a rather empty world, for there weren't many of these people. In all of France, where today there are more than 50 million people, there were probably no more than 50 thousand Cro-Magnons. They probably lived in little groups of 20 or 30, and like the Neanderthals, they were hunters. In Europe, they hunted horses, bison, cave bears, woolly rhinoceroses, mammoths, and most of all, the vast herds of reindeer that roamed southern Europe during the Ice Age. The hunters and their families followed the herds back and forth for hundreds of miles, staying at times in caves, pitching animal-skin tents in the shelter of cliffs, or camping where water was available beside lakes, rivers, and ponds.

Of course, the Cro-Magnons were not just physically different from the Neanderthals—they were mentally different as well. They were more intelligent. Whereas the Neanderthals had lived for many thousands of years without doing much more than just improving their tools and weapons, Cro-Magnons came up with scores of new ideas. One of their first inventions was a way of chipping flint. Unlike the Neanderthals who could get only a few tools out of a chunk of flint, the Cro-Magnons could get dozens. They had discovered how to flake a chunk of flint into many slim, sharp-edged blades that could be turned into spearpoints, scrapers, chisels, knives, and a variety of other tools.

As time went on, Cro-Magnon people invented a number of other things. One was a device that hasn't changed in 20 thousand years—the needle. Cro-Magnon needles were made of thin slivers of bone shaped with flint tools. It's obvious that Cro-Magnons must have used these needles to make *sewn* clothing, and indeed, a little carved ivory statue made by a Cro-Magnon artist shows us what that clothing was like. Made during one of the cold periods, it depicts a man wearing a warm-looking, one-piece fur suit with a hood.

Another invention was the first kind of lamp—a scooped-out stone bowl filled with animal grease, in which floated a burning wick of moss or twisted fur. And these people also invented a new, faster way of starting fires by striking a piece of iron ore with a piece of flint to make hot sparks.

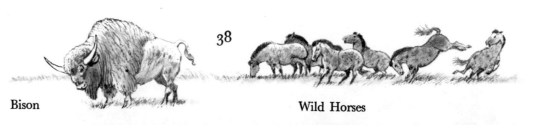

Bison

Wild Horses

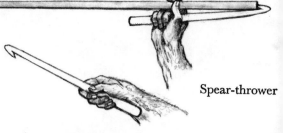

Spear-thrower

Many inventions had to do with ways of killing animals more efficiently. An invention that helped make the Cro-Magnons mighty hunters was the spear-thrower—a hooked rod that was used like a catapult, enabling a man to throw a spear farther, harder, and more accurately than ever before. Later came harpoons made of reindeer antler and bone, with rows of hooked barbs on their edges. And still later came the invention of the bow and arrow, and the fishhook.

Bone flutes and whistles found in caves show that the Cro-Magnons were probably the world's first musicians. They evidently were also the world's first artists and craftsmen. They made necklaces of snail shells and animal teeth, and pendants of bone with pictures of animals scratched into them. Cro-Magnon artists also made little carved statues of stone, clay, and bone, as well as carvings on rock walls of animals and of fat women that may have represented a goddess they worshipped. The Cro-Magnons of France and Spain, about 18 to 13 thousand years ago, painted beautiful, lifelike animals on the walls of caves and decorated their tools and weapons with realistic carvings of animals and birds. These people also left us one carved, painted portrait that shows what they looked like. It is of a light-skinned, snub-nosed man with black hair and a black beard. Of course, like us, Cro-Magnons probably had different skin colors, differently shaped eyes, and slightly different body shapes, depending on where in the world they lived.

From paintings and statues, tools and weapons, ornaments and belongings, anthropologists have been able to put together a clear picture of the Cro-Magnons. We can see that they were a smart, skillful people who invented and discovered many ways of making themselves more comfortable and secure in a still savage world. They were moving along the path that led to civilization. By 10 thousand years ago, their descendants were the world's first farmers, tamers of animals, and citizens of settled communities.

Primitive Bone Whistle

Stone Statue
(The Gagarino Venus)

Gastropod Shell Necklace

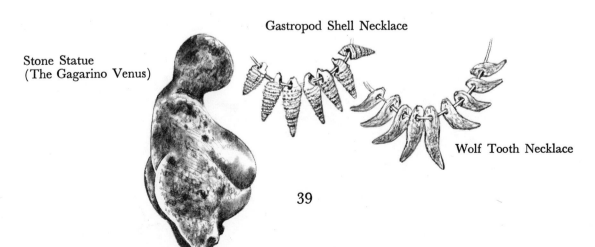

Wolf Tooth Necklace

39

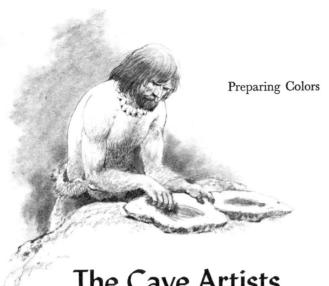

Preparing Colors

The Cave Artists

THE CAVE wound down into the earth—a series of twisting tunnels, nooks, crannies, and chambers. Slowly, it had been carved out during tens of thousands of years by the water of a million rains trickling down through the rock, each drop carrying away a tiny bit of dissolved material. No beam of sunlight had ever reached into most of these tunnels and caverns, nor ever would. They lay in the pitch-blackness of never-ending night. They lay in silence, too, except for the faint, distant drip-drip-drip from some remote pit where the water was still at work, patiently forming yet another cavern.

But in one chamber of the cave there was both sound and light. Tiny, trembling glows edged feebly out into the darkness, drawing small sparkles and gleams from the humped rocks. The light came from the flaring wicks of a trio of crude lamps that sat on a rocky ledge jutting out of the cavern's limestone wall. They were hollowed stone slabs filled with smoking, smelly animal grease, and they flickered to the soft whisper of a wad of fur being rubbed over rock. For in the dim radiance, a man was working, perched on the rocky ledge where he could reach high up on the wall. He was a bearded, long-haired man wearing gar-ments of animal skin and a necklace of sea-shells. Into a hand-held container, he dipped the fur wad, bringing it forth glistening with color. He then rubbed the fur onto the wall. Under his skilled strokes, a shape was emerging.

After a time, the man seemed satisfied with his work. He clambered down to the floor of the cavern and stood, gazing up at the patch of wall on which he had been working. On the yellowish stone, a great, hump-necked brown bison stood, the newest addition to the parade of animals that marched across the wall. As the lamp flick-ered, the animals seemed almost to move and breathe.

The man moved back to the wall and picked up several objects, together with one of the three lamps. Blowing out the other two flames, he turned, and ducking his head, he began the difficult climb through a narrow tunnel back up to the light of day. Behind him, total darkness flowed into the cavern.

When paintings made on cave walls by prehistoric artists of 10 to 20 thousand years ago were first discovered, most people did not believe they were genuine. They are as skillfully done and as beautiful as many

Stone Lamp

paintings by artists of today. It didn't seem possible that primitive, fur-clad "savages" could have done such things. But as other decorated caves were discovered—caves that had been sealed for thousands of years —it became obvious that the paintings had indeed been done by prehistoric people. For the pictures showed animals that no present-day person had ever seen. On the walls and ceilings of scores of caves in Spain and France, artists of long ago left amazing scenes showing animals of their times. Herds of shaggy horses gallop, giant woolly mammoths lumber, great bisons snort and paw the earth, cave lions prowl, deer run. Many of these animals are now gone from the earth forever. But because of these marvelous paintings by people who knew them as living creatures, we know what these extinct animals looked like.

Paintings of animals were not the only kind of art that prehistoric people left in caves. They also left drawings scratched on rock walls, sculptures carved in rock, prints of human hands, and strange, swirling designs.

The swirling designs were made by people dragging their fingertips through damp clay on cave walls, leaving grooves that would still be there many thousands of years later. The people ran their fingers in long, straight lines, and curves, and they swirled them around to make circles. There is no way to tell if these designs were made for a reason, or just for fun.

The handprints were made by holding a hand against the rock wall and blowing paint at it through a bone tube. This left

the shape of a hand on the wall, outlined in red or black. Again, we do not know if this had some meaning for the Ice Age people, or if it was done just for amusement.

Ice Age artists scratched pictures of animals on cave walls using pieces of flint that were chipped into chisellike points. One of these tools was found just where an artist put it down some 20 thousand years ago on a stone ledge in a cave beneath a beautiful scratch drawing of a cave lion.

But of all the forms of prehistoric art, paintings are the most beautiful. There are several kinds. One kind is simple, colored outlines or shapes of animals painted in red, yellow, or black. Others are much more realistic. The artists used different shades of color to make the animals seem more rounded, often painting them over bumps in the walls to help create a feeling of roundness and muscles.

The cave painters got most of their paint colors from the earth. Certain kinds of soft rocks are red, brown, orange, and yellow. And to make their paints, prehistoric artists ground such rocks to a powder on flat slabs of stone, mixing the powders with grease made of animal fat. This produced a thick, pasty paint that was apparently usually kept in large seashells or in hollow tubes of bone. Stone grinding slabs, and shells and tubes with faint traces of paint still in them, have been found.

The artists may have smeared the paint onto the cave walls with their fingers, or they may have used crude brushes of wadded fur. Some parts of paintings look as if they were made with a kind of stamping

tool—a piece of bone or wood wrapped in animal skin. The end of the tool was then dipped into paint and pressed against the cave wall.

Today, artists often make sketches before they do a finished painting. Prehistoric artists may have done this, too. Pieces of flat stone have been found with drawings scratched on them that match the paintings in some of the caves. Were these, perhaps, prehistoric "sketch pads?"

There are many questions about cave paintings, but the biggest one is, What were they for? Some of them are near the entrances of caves where people may have lived, so perhaps those paintings were decorations. But a great many of the paintings and sculptures are in deep, dark parts of caves that are very hard to get to. Often they are tucked away in hidden corners, and even in pits. It seems as if the artists deliberately put these paintings in places where they could not easily be seen. Surely if these paintings were decorations, they wouldn't have been hidden away.

Many anthropologists think that these painted caves were used for magic rites. Next to some of the paintings are marks that look as if they are meant to be spears or arrows flying at the animals. Some of the pictures are even scarred, as though they had been stabbed with the points of weapons. Perhaps these dark, hidden parts of caves were secret places where hunters went for magical ceremonies that they believed would give them power to find and kill the animals painted on the walls. There, where flickering firelight shimmered on the stone, the men may have danced and chanted and thrust their spears at the animal pictures.

But other anthropologists doubt this. They suggest that although the painted caves may be hard to get to *now*, this might not have been the case 20 or 30 thousand years ago. Then, the caves may have had entrances that made them easy to get into —entrances that have since become blocked. And these anthropologists also point out that many of the "arrows" look as if they are *missing* the animals they are supposed to be flying at. Perhaps they aren't supposed to be arrows at all—perhaps they stand for wind or rain.

The fact is, we don't really know what these paintings illustrate, or why prehistoric artists even painted them. It may have been for magic; it may have been for decoration; it may have been for fun. It may have been for all three. Or, it may have been for some reason we can't even imagine! But one thing *is* sure—many of these paintings are great pieces of art, and the artists who painted them deserve to be counted among the greatest painters in the world!

The Ice Age Americans

ON A BROAD PLAIN beneath a sullen sky that hinted at a coming blizzard, a herd of reindeer grazed.

Twenty yards away from the herd, the leader of a band of hunters crept slowly forward, moving on his thigh and elbow. His stomach ached with hunger, but he forced himself to move by inches, lest the animals be startled and run. He and the other hunters, who were spread out in a broad semicircle abreast of him, had been closing in on the herd for nearly an hour, taking advantage of every stunted bush and bump in the landscape to keep their movements hidden. To the reindeer, the hunters appeared to be animals like themselves, for each man wore reindeer antlers on his head, tied on with leather thongs. Even so, too quick a movement could startle the whole herd into flight.

So the leader inched his way forward, stopping motionless and averting his eyes whenever one of the reindeer looked his way. The animals on the outskirts of the herd were nervous, and from time to time, one or more of them would pause in its feeding and stare suspiciously at the men creeping toward them.

Slowly, the leader lessened the distance between himself and the nearest animals, and finally, he judged that he was near enough. With the slightest movement of his head, he checked the positions of his hunters. They, too, were in place. Gently, he drew back his spear, tensing his body for a throw.

Perhaps a whiff of the hunters' smell reached the animals, for the nearest reindeer tossed its head and snorted to clear its nostrils for a better scent. But a moment later, it was shuddering on the ground, the leader's stone-tipped spear buried deep in its neck.

The sudden tang of blood that filled the air and the sudden flash of motion of the hunters' arms as they cast their weapons triggered the herd into instant flight. But two of the animals were left behind, sprawled on the hard, half-frozen ground, their eyes glazing in death.

The antlered men hurried forward, little plumes of vapor spurting from their mouths and noses in the brisk, cold air. They lashed the animals' front and back legs together and slung each beast over a stout pole made of a trimmed tree branch they had brought with them. With two men carrying each pole, the hunters turned and headed back

toward the spot where their hungry women and children were anxiously awaiting them, several miles behind.

The two dead reindeer would keep them all fed for a couple of days, then the hunters would again face the need to find food. But this was no problem as far as the leader and his men were concerned, for the reindeer herd was moving on ahead of them, and all they had to do was follow after it.

That night, the hunters and their families filled their bellies again. The skins of the reindeer were scraped clean and packed into bundles, and the uneaten flesh of the animals was cut up and packed away as well. The next morning, with the first light of dawn, the people were on their way again, following the reindeer.

This was the Ice Age, and across much of the northern part of the world, great sheets of ice, thousands of feet thick, covered thousands and thousands of miles. The bulk of these ice masses was made up of water that had come from the sea. Billions of tons of gray ocean had gone into the icy monsters, and because of this, the seas of the world were much lower than they had been before the Ice Age began. In many places, the lowering of the water had exposed the tops of underwater mountains and hills, and in one place, a broad, flat plain had emerged from the sea to form a wide bridge of land between the continents of Asia and North America. In fact, the plain on which the reindeer hunters were following the herd actually was this bridge, and eventually, drifting slowly eastward, one such group of hunters moved off the bridge and became the first humans in North America.

What were these people like? They were Ice Age people of Asia—Cro-Magnons—much like the people of Europe. Their descendants would become the American Indians! Many scientists think these people were already much like Indians, with broad faces, high cheekbones, and big teeth. And, they were probably dressed much like Eskimos, in hooded garments of animal skins.

No one is sure just when the first Ice Age Asians arrived in North America, but it was probably between 20 and 30 thousand years ago. They came into the part of North America that is now Alaska. For a time, they could go no further, because in the north, east, and south lay huge sheets of ice, grimly barring the way.

In the years that followed, groups of nomadic hunters and their families almost certainly continued to cross the land bridge, and the number of people who lived and hunted in North America grew. After many generations, the world became warmer, and the ice sheets began to melt and shrink. A pathway south opened up, and animals found their way to it, moving to new grazing lands. Naturally, some of the nomadic hunters followed them.

And so, the hunters entered a vast land of fertile plains and thick forests filled with a host of animals—deer, antelope, bear, rabbit, horses, small camels, big bison, giant mastodons, and woolly mammoths. It was a hunter's paradise. And of course there were seeds, nuts, fruits, and edible roots and plants to be gathered.

Just as the Ice Age people of the Old

World were learning new things, so, too, were the Ice Age Americans. The first people who came from Asia probably had stone or bone-tipped spears and cutting tools of chipped stone. Their descendants, the people of 12 thousand years ago, had spear-throwers, and beautifully made, deadly spearpoints of flint, obsidian, and other easily chipped minerals. These points, which have been found in all parts of North America, were from 4 to 6 inches long, usually with notches chipped into their bases where they fitted onto wooden shafts. With these weapons, the ancient Americans hunted the biggest animals of their world—the great, elephantlike mastodons and mammoths. This is known because skeletons of these giant beasts have been found with these spearpoints in them. The hunters probably wounded the animals by throwing spears at them, then trailed them until they weakened enough to be rushed and killed. In some cases, the hunters apparently stampeded the creatures over the edges of cliffs or trapped them in bogs.

Of course, other animals were hunted, too—horses, camels, giant sloths, antelope, and a huge kind of shaggy bison that is now extinct. Many skeletons of these bison have been found with spearpoints in them, but the spearpoints are broader and shorter than the others, and they were probably made by people who lived a thousand or more years after the makers of the first points.

Like the prehistoric people of Europe, Asia, and Africa, the Ice Age Americans made things other than weapons. They produced beads made of bone, stone, and snail shells. Some of them made a kind of rope from the twisted leaves of sagebrush, and with this rope they wove baskets. They also made sandals of sagebrush rope, some of which were found remarkably well preserved in the dry air of a cave in Oregon. Ten thousand years old, they are the oldest-known footwear in the world. And in the state of Washington, bone needles have been found that are as slim and fine as those now made of steel.

Generation after generation, groups of Ice Age Americans continued to move south, east, and north. By 12 thousand years ago, they were in every part of North America, and by 10 thousand years ago—or earlier—they had reached lower South America. These little groups of Ice Age people, living throughout North, Central, and South America, became the tribes of American Indians.

Giant Sloth (Megatherium)

Small Antelope

47

American Camel

The Great Change

A BRIGHT, early morning sun was chasing the night's shadows out of a hilly landscape. From a tiny cluster of mud houses on one of the hills overlooking a small lake, a group of women, young girls, and small children, all dressed in garments of animal hide, made their way out onto the hillside, spreading out as they went. Many of them carried baskets woven of dried grass.

One of the girls was in her twelfth summer. Ever since she had been very small, she had come out with the other girls and women each day during the spring, summer, and autumn to search for seeds, roots, berries, and other plant food that could be eaten by her people. Such things were an important addition to the meat the village men brought in from their hunting. Sometimes, if the hunting did not go well, the plant food the women found was the main source of food.

So, from earliest childhood, the girl had probably spent a good part of her life with her back bent and her eyes on the ground. She had learned much, both from the older women and from the earth itself. She knew which berries were sweet and which bitter, which mushrooms could be eaten and which might cause death. She knew which plants had fat, tasty roots and which had pleasant tasting seeds.

But on this day, there would be no need to do any searching. The tall, slender spiky-topped plants that grew so thickly on the hillsides had come into their time of ripeness. For the next two or three weeks, the women would be working nearly from dawn until dusk, first cutting off the tops of the plants, then extracting the brown, ripe seeds from the spikes. This was food that could be dried and stored away for a long time, to be used when needed. Putting down her basket, the girl went to work, grasping clusters of stalks in one hand and slicing through them with a wooden tool armed with bits of sharp stone.

Just as it is today with the women and girls of Bushmen families of Africa who gather plant food while their men hunt, so it probably was with the women and girls of prehistoric times. They, too, were the gatherers of plant food. And it was from thousands of years of such plant-food gathering, in places where certain kinds of plants grew, that the idea of farming—of purposely planting seeds to make useful or edible plants grow—was born.

About 11 thousand years ago, in that part

Barley

Wheat

of the Near East where Turkey, Syria, Iraq, Iran, and Israel now lie, there were little, scattered villages of people who were slowly becoming the world's first farmers. These people were probably much like those who live in these places today—rather short, with tan-colored skin and dark hair and eyes. In some places, these people lived in villages of square or beehive-shaped houses made of dried-mud bricks. In other places, they lived in underground, stone-lined huts. And in still other places, these people lived in villages of circular huts all connected together like a honeycomb.

In the places where these villages were, everything was just right for farming. There was enough rain to make many kinds of grasses grow, and yet not enough rain to let trees flourish and shut out the light needed by the grasses. As a result, several kinds of grasses grew thickly on the hillsides, and some of them were the ancestors of the wheat and barley that are so important to the world today. It was the fruit of these grasses—grain—that was one of the most vital foods the women of the villages gathered. They cut it with crude sickles made from straight or sometimes curved pieces of bone or wood into which many little, sharp-edged pieces of flint were wedged. This gave the sickle a sharp cutting edge.

Animals abounded in most of these places, too. There were herds of wild sheep, goats, and cattle, and families of wild hogs —all animals the village men hunted. But in thousands of years, they would become tame farm animals.

We cannot tell exactly where, when, or how farming first began, but it started somewhere in the lands of the Near East about 9 thousand years ago. And, since women were the food gatherers, experienced in the ways of plants, it was almost certainly women who were the very first farmers.

Farming would not have been any sudden, miraculous discovery. It must have taken generations. First, probably long before they even lived in villages, women must have learned that plants *grew* from seeds. Later, the women may have helped certain plants grow by spreading some of their seeds around. And still later, they may have helped these plants flourish by pulling up weeds that struggled with the plants for growing space. Slowly, the village hillsides would have become filled mainly with the kinds of plants the women wanted.

The same sort of thing may have happened with animals. The hunters, wise in the ways of the beasts they hunted, may have tried to kill mainly very young or very old animals, leaving the prime males and females to breed. If hunting-animals such as wolves or lions moved into the neighborhood, the men probably killed them off as quickly as possible to protect the herd animals. In this way, even though the herds of sheep, goats, and cattle provided food for the humans, the humans might have helped them to flourish.

Some people think that some of the human hunters occasionally hunted large groups of animals, driving them into places where they could be penned and kept until

Beans

Squash

Millet

they were needed for food. If some of these captive animals had babies, the young ones, growing up near humans instead of in the wild, might have become more tame. Perhaps it was from such animals, born in captivity, that the first herds of livestock were formed. The very first farm animals were sheep, tamed by people of the Near East between 10 and 11 thousand years ago.

The grain that the first farmers harvested was not ground into flour and baked into bread as it is now. That discovery would not be made for several thousand years more. Instead, the first farmers cracked the brown kernels of wheat and barley by crushing them with round stones in stone bowls and then heated them in crude, pitlike ovens to dry them out. The dried, cracked grain was then mixed with water to make a gritty kind of porridge, much like a crunchy, nutty breakfast cereal. Tasty and nutritious, this sort of food is still eaten in many places today.

Farming was not invented just once in only one place—it was invented many times by people thousands of miles apart who never even dreamed that other people existed. About 6 thousand years ago, people in China began to grow the grain called millet. And in Mexico, about 8 thousand years ago, people were growing squash, beans, and later, corn.

From each of the places where the invention of farming occurred, news of its practice slowly spread out. Knowledge of how to grow corn moved down into South America and up into parts of North America. Knowledge of how to grow millet, and later rice, spread throughout Asia. From the Near East, the idea of growing wheat and barley was carried up into Europe, now warming up after the melting of the glaciers, and then on into Africa.

Everywhere, life changed. People who had lived by hunting began to clear away the forests to make room for fields of grain. In different parts of the world, various kinds of animals were tamed and became livestock. Pottery was invented, and grain was stored in great clay bowls and jars. The plough was invented, and farmers began to plant their crops in straight rows that made weeding and harvesting easier. They even discovered how to irrigate their fields by digging ditches from nearby streams.

The invention of farming changed the world for humans. It was as important as learning to make tools and use fire. For with farming and villages came the beginning of civilization.

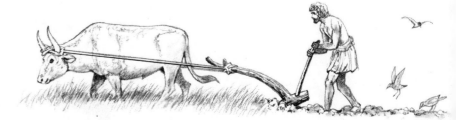

Tombs, Temples, and Standing Stones

STEP—HEAVE! Step—heave!

The young, red-bearded man moved in regular rhythm with the hundreds of men stretched out before and behind him. Clutching a rope of twisted leather, he took a short step forward, digging his foot sharply into the ground and then *heaving* with all the strength of his arms and shoulders.

The rope stretched back several hundred feet to where it was tied to a log platform. On the platform lay an immense, oblong stone, three times longer than a man. For 40 days, "Redbeard" and a thousand other men, hauling on ropes attached to the platform, sweated and strained to drag the giant stone across the plain. While he and the others kept up their steady step-heave advance, groups of other men worked at laying stout, smooth logs in the platform's path for it to roll on. As the stone slid over each log, the log was picked up by a crew of workers and carried forward to be placed in front of the platform again.

"Redbeard" let go of the rope with one hand for a moment, to wipe the sweat from his face with the back of his arm. For some time now he had been able to see, far in the distance, the stone's destination. In another ten days or so, they would be there.

Until then . . . he gripped the rope once more. Step—heave! Step—heave!

The men who hauled that giant stone over the plain lived about 3,500 years ago. The place to which they dragged the stone still stands on that plain in England. It is a puzzle out of the past, a mysterious huddle of huge, gray, stone slabs that has come to be known as *Stonehenge*. Thousands of years ago, prehistoric people—people who still dressed in garments of animal skin, who had only just begun to practice a primitive kind of farming, and who had only tools made of stone and bone, leather and wood —set up these great stones for some purpose we can now only guess at.

Many of the big slabs have fallen down, but it is still possible to see how they all once formed a strange sort of design. Thirty of them stood in a big circle with other stones lying flat across their tops to form a continuous ring. Inside the circle was another circle of smaller stones, and inside that was a half-circle of the very biggest stones of all. They were arranged in pairs, with stone slabs lying across the tops of each pair so that they looked like doorways of a giant's castle. All this stood in the middle of a great, flat circle of ground surrounded

THE CONSTRUCTION OF STONEHENGE

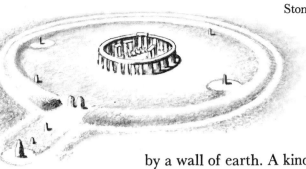

by a wall of earth. A kind of broad avenue, 40 feet wide, led up to the walled circle.

Some of the great stones that make up Stonehenge are as much as 20 feet long and weigh more than 40 tons. Even today, with cranes, engines, and power tools, it wouldn't be easy to set such stones upright and lay other big stones on top of them. Yet, the people who built this structure between 3 and 4 thousand years ago had only stone hammers, pickaxes made of deer antlers, and shovels made of the shoulder bones of oxen. With these tools they cut and trimmed big chunks of stone from a sandstone hill to the size and shape they wanted, then hauled them by hand 24 miles to the place where they were set up.

There, pits were dug, and the stones were placed with their ends hanging over the pits. Using logs as great levers and braces, and tugging on ropes, the men eased the big stones into the pits which were then filled with dirt to hold the stones in place. And none of this was done by chance or guesswork. The prehistoric people who built Stonehenge used mathematics to make their circles perfect and to make the spaces between the stones equal.

What was this great design of giant stones that was so carefully planned and that took so much time and effort to build? No one knows for sure, but it seems as if Stonehenge had something to do with the sun, the moon, and the seasons. For on one special day each year, something wonderful happens in the ancient circle of stones.

Some distance outside the outer ring, in the broad avenue, two big stones stand side

by side with a narrow space between them. Farther back in the avenue stands a single pointed boulder. When someone stands in the middle of the ring of stones and faces east, they look straight between the two stones at the pointed boulder. And on the first day of summer, every year, the sun rises directly from behind that boulder! First, the sky grows pale. Then, suddenly, the tip of the boulder glows as if it is on fire. Slowly, the fiery circle of the sun moves up until it seems to be balanced on the boulder's pointed end. Its pink rays come marching down the broad avenue and flow into the circle of stones.

Obviously, Stonehenge was designed so that this would happen. Was Stonehenge a temple for worshipping the sun? Were great ceremonies held here each year, on the morning of the first day of summer, to honor the time of year when plants grow and animals are plentiful? Maybe.

Stonehenge isn't the only great stone structure that has been left to us by these people of four, five, and six thousand years ago. There are many others. A few are as mysterious as Stonehenge. Rings of boulders of various shapes and sizes are found in many parts of England, Scotland, and Wales. Only 17 miles from Stonehenge are the remains of a giant ring of stones that had several smaller rings inside it, and two long, winding avenues of standing stones leading to it. In France, prehistoric people set up 2,700 big boulders in long, straight rows—row after row—covering nearly 4 square miles all together. And in many places stand single giant stones, sometimes with strange designs chiseled on them.

While the purposes of these rings, rows, and standing stones are still a mystery, the functions of the other stone structures from the past are known. They are tombs and temples. On the island of Malta, in the Mediterranean Sea, are the remains of the first stone temples in the world. They were built about 5 thousand years ago and were constructed of great boulders, carefully fitted together and sometimes covered with painted plaster. In one of them, there was a great stone statue of a hugely fat woman —a goddess. Smaller statues of this goddess have been found in many other parts of Europe. Apparently, she was worshipped for many thousands of years.

Dotting the countrysides in many parts of England, Scotland, Ireland, France, Spain, Holland, Germany, Sweden, and Denmark are tens of thousands of stone tombs. Some of them are 6 thousand years old, the oldest stone monuments in the world. Many of the tombs are simply one-room chambers with walls and ceilings made of piled-together stones. Some are single chambers with long tunnels leading into them. Others are like big halls with ceilings and walls made of huge slabs and boulders. Most of these structures were covered over with earth, so that with time, they became great, green mounds and hills. On the rock walls of some of them, the builders chiseled strange designs—zigzags, swirls, and rayed circles that may stand for the sun. Most of these tombs are actually cemeteries in which many generations of people were buried, often with tools, cups, ornaments, and other things that had probably belonged to them in life.

The quality of the thinking behind these ancient structures—the stone tombs of Europe, the temples of Malta, and the great rows and circles of stones in England—tell us that the skin-clad people who built them with their crude tools of stone and bone were far from being mere, rough savages. On the contrary, they were just as capable of working out ways of doing things and solving problems as we are.

Metal and Marks in Clay

IN A SHALLOW PIT that had been dug in the dirt floor of a small, dried-mud building, a mass of burning coals glowed. Sitting atop the coals was a thick, clay bowl filled with reddish-brown chunks. Around the pit squatted four men, each with a long, hollow reed that had been cut from the bank of a nearby river. Through these tubes, the men blew steadily into the fire, producing a constant flow of air that fanned the coals into a hot, orange glare.

Abruptly, in the clay pot, there was a quiver. Shimmering, the chunks of reddish-brown stuff dissolved into a bright, gleaming liquid.

Quickly, the men set their tubes aside. Two of them picked up lengths of wood—peeled branches of young, green shrubs that had been soaking in water. Placing a stick along each side of the clay bowl and squeezing both ends of the sticks together, the men used them as tongs, lifting the bowl out of the coals. Slowly, very carefully, the men sidled toward a small, square chunk of sandstone that stood nearby. Gently, they tilted the bowl so that the bright liquid poured into a shape that was cut into the sandstone. They poured until the liquid was even with the top of the block.

When the two men moved away, another man came to squat over the sandstone block. He watched it intently for a few minutes, and when he was sure the liquid had hardened, he picked up the block and carried it to a large, stone slab. Turning the block upside down, he gave it several sharp shakes. With a clink, an object fell from the block onto the slab. It was a perfectly shaped, pointed spearhead—molded of gleaming copper.

For hundreds of thousands of years, humanity's most important material for tools had been stone. But by about 6 thousand years ago, humans had begun to use the material that would replace stone forever—cast metal.

The first metal used by people was copper—the shiny, reddish-brown stuff that our pennies and electrical wires are mostly made of today. Now, our copper comes from ores that are mined. But when people first began to use it, lumps of pure copper could be found in many places on the surface of the earth, and people may have discovered them while looking for brightly colored rocks to make into paint. Prehistoric people used red and yellow ocher, and other kinds of soft rock for paint, breaking

CASTING COPPER SPEARHEAD

them up and grinding them into powder. But if they attempted to do this with a lump of shiny copper, in trying to break up the metal, they would have found that it could be hammered into simple shapes and thin sheets.

Prehistoric people knew about copper at least 12 thousand years ago. In the Near East, artists were then hammering beads and pendants out of the metal. But it wasn't for many thousands of years that they learned how to form it into shapes by melting it and pouring it into molds.

The molding and casting of copper was the beginning. By about 5 thousand years ago, in the Near East, metalworkers learned to mix copper with tin to make bronze, an artificial metal that was tougher and harder than either tin or copper alone. Thus, humans were no longer depending on the materials they could simply find—they were creating their own materials.

By that time, cities and kingdoms had risen in many parts of the world. The wheel had been invented, giving rise to carts, wagons, and chariots—the first of humanity's wheeled vehicles. Fat-bodied ships manned by swarthy sailors were gliding through the warm Mediterranean Sea carrying metal tools, blue glass beads, and other trade goods. These ships also carried *ideas*. Knowledge of smelting and casting metals, of making wheels, of better ways of farming, and of better methods of building all spread throughout the Mediterranean area.

Also at about this time, in the land of Sumer where southern Iraq lies today, short, stocky, dark-eyed men sat cross-legged, making rows of crude little pictures with wooden sticks on flattened lumps of wet clay. The pictures stood for words in the Sumerian language. Writing had been invented. A new age had truly begun.

The long, upward climb that began with the apelike creatures who left the trees and moved out onto the plains had now reached wheels, metal, writing, and civilization. The climb would continue, sometimes swiftly, sometimes with little pauses. But knowledge would gather and grow until 5 thousand years after humans first began to write, other humans would actually be able to leave their world to probe hundreds of thousands of black, airless miles of space, thus widening their understanding of the universe—a feat as marvelous as the making of the first tool.

And, we hope, the climb is far from over. We're still climbing. If we stay on the path our prehistoric ancestors followed, we can continue to learn, to discover, and to understand more about ourselves, our world, and our universe.

Pronunciation Guide

Aegyptopithecus	(ee-JIP-tuh-PITH-ik-uhs)
Australopithecine	(AW-struh-loh-PITH-uh-seen)
Australopithecus afarensis	(AW-struh-loh-PITH-uh-kuhs ah-fah-REN-sis)
Australopithecus africanus	(AW-struh-loh-PITH-uh-kuhs ah-free-KAHN-uhs)
Australopithecus boisei	(AW-struh-loh-PITH-uh-kuhs BOYZ-ee-eye)
Australopithecus robustus	(AW-struh-loh-PITH-uh-kuhs roh-BUS-tuhs)
Cro-Magnon	(kro-MAG-nuhn)
Hominid	(HAHM-ih-nihd)
Hominidae	(hoh-MIN-uh-dee)
Homo erectus	(hoh-moh ee-REKT-uhs)
Homo habilis	(hoh-moh HAB-il-ihs)
Homo sapiens	(hoh-moh SAYP-ee-enz)
Neanderthal	(nee-AN-der-thawl)
Primate	(PRY-mayt)
Prosimian	(proh-SIM-ee-uhn)
Ramapithecus	(ram-uh-PITH-uh-cuhs)

Index

Aegypytopithecus, 15
American Indians, 46-7
Anatomy, 11; defined, 28
Antelopes, 23, 46-7
Anthropologist, defined, 10
Apes, 10-11, 14, 18-19
Art, prehistoric, 39-43
Australopithecines, 11, 20-23, 26
Australopithecus afarensis, 18-19, 22-3
Australopithecus africanus, 21-3
Australopithecus boisei, 22, 23
Australopithecus robustus, 22, 23

Baboons, 20, 27
Barley, 50-1
Baskets, 47-8
Beans, 51
Bears, 27, 31, 34, 38, 46
Beaver, 28
Bison, 38, 40, 42, 46-7
Boar, 27
Bronze, 58
Burial of the dead, 28-9, 31, 55
Bushmen of Africa, 48

Camels, 27, 46-7
Cats, 27
Cattle, 50
Cave bears, 31, 34, 38
Cave dwelling, 32-3, 43
Cave painting, 39, 40-3
Chimpanzees, 11, 15
Clothing, 26, 30, 32, 38, 40, 46, 48-9, 52
Copper, 56-8
Corn, 51
Cro-Magnon people, 11, 17, 19, 36-9, 44-7

Dating methods, scientific, 11
Deer, 8, 27, 42, 46

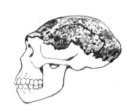

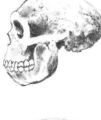

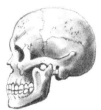

Elephants, 24–7, 35
Evolution, described, 14–15; illustrated, 17

Farming, 48–52
Fire, use of, 8–10, 24–33, 36, 38, 40, 56
Flamingos, 20
Flint, 26, 28, 30, 32, 36–8, 42, 47, 50
Foxes, 27

Gagarino Venus, 39
Gazelles, 23
Giant sloth, 47
Gibbons, 14, 15
Glaciers, 32, 34–5, 46
Goats, 50
Gorillas, 11, 15, 20, 22
Grain, 48–51

Hippopotamus, 35
Hogs, wild, 50
Hominids, defined, 12
Hominids (Hominidae), 12, 14–23
Homo erectus, 17, 19, 24–7
Homo habilis, 17, 19, 23
Homo Neanderthal, 19
Homo sapiens, defined, 10
Homo sapiens Neanderthalensis, 17
Homo sapiens sapiens, 17
Horses, 27, 38, 42, 46–7
Human, defined, 10
Hunting, 23, 24–7, 32, 38–9, 44–8, 50–1
Hyenas, 21, 23

Ice Age, 30, 32–5, 38, 42, 44–7
Ice sheets, 32, 34–5, 46
Irrigation, 51

Jewelry, 36, 39–40, 47, 58

Lamps, 38, 40–1
Land bridge, 46
Language, 10–11, 27, 58
Lemurs, 14
Lions, 20, 23, 42, 50
"Lucy," 18–19

Magic, 31, 43
Mammoths, 32, 34–5, 38, 42, 46–7
Mastodons, 46–7
Mathematics, 54
Metalworking, 56–8
Millet, 51
Monkeys, 10–11, 14
Musical instruments, 39
Musk oxen, 34

Neanderthal people, 11, 17, 19, 28–31, 35, 38
Needles, 38, 47
Nomads, 9, 27, 46
"Nutcracker man," 22

Orangutans, 15
Ornaments, 31, 39, 55, 58
Ovens, 51

Plough, 51
Pottery, 51, 56
Primates, 10, 11, 14–15
Prosimians, 14–15

Rabbits, 14, 26
Ramapithecus, 12–15
Reindeer, 34, 36, 38, 44–6
Religion, 31, 39, 55
Rhinoceros, 8, 20, 27, 34, 38
Rice, 51
Rope, 47, 52

Saber-toothed cats, 20, 23, 24
Sailing, 58
Sandals, 47
Sculpture, 38–9, 43, 55
Sheep, 50–1
Shelter, 27, 28–30, 32–3, 36–8, 48–50
Spear-thrower, 39, 47
Species, defined, 14
Squash, 51
Stonehenge, 52–4

Tarsiers, 14
Temples, 54–5
Tombs, 55
Tools, 8–11, 23, 24–7, 30–1, 36, 38–9, 42–3, 47–58
Trade, 58

Vultures, 21, 23

Water buffalo, 27
Weapons, 24–7, 30–1, 38–9, 43–7, 56
Wheat, 50–1
Wheel, 58
Wolves, 34, 50
Writing, invention of, 58

Zebras, 20